The Stowaway Fairy
Written and Illustrated by Mary Koski

Book design by Paul Turley

Island Heritage Publishing
Copyright © 1991
First Edition, Fourth Printing 1995

Address orders and correspondence to:

 ISLAND HERITAGE PUBLISHING
A division of The Madden Corporation
99-880 Iwaena Street
Aiea, Hawaii 96701
(808) 487-7299

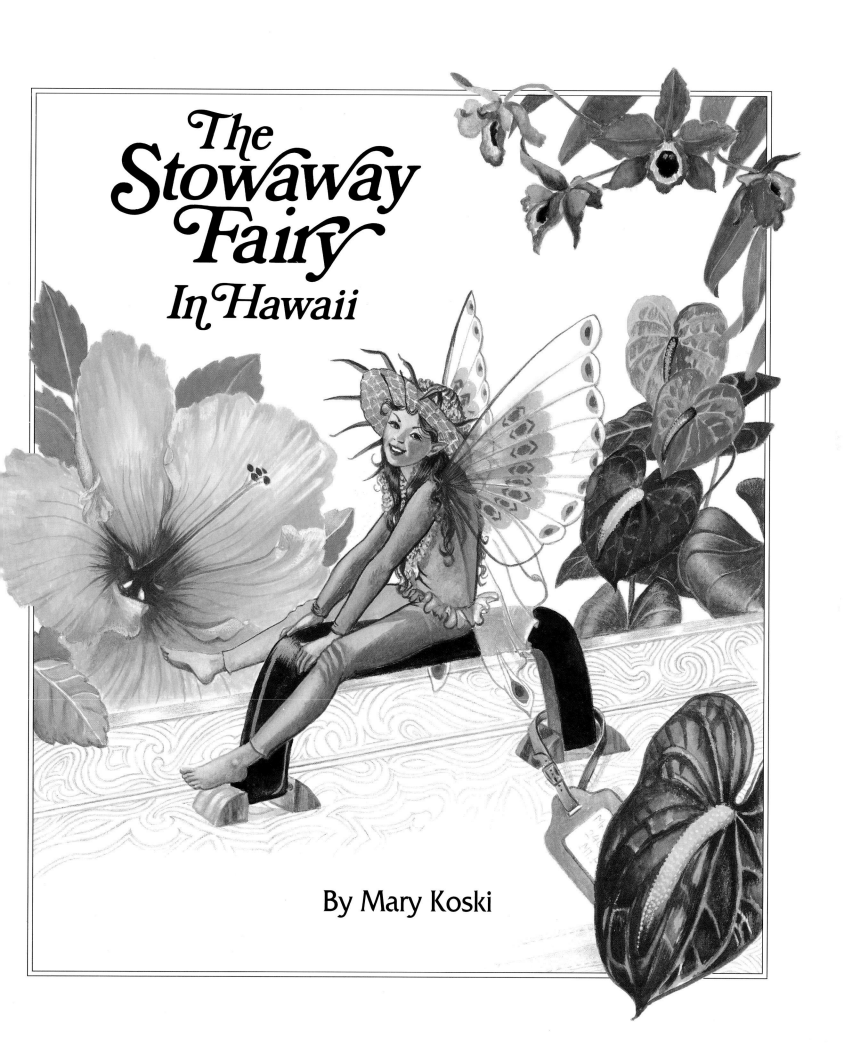

The Stowaway Fairy
In Hawaii

By Mary Koski

2

"Golly! What's that?" wondered Rosie the garden fairy, peeking through the window of the house in front of her garden. She thought she had spotted some red and lavender flowers in a box, but she wasn't sure. "I'll just have to get into the house for a closer look," she said to herself.

It was cold and snowy in Vermont, and Rosie should have been sleeping. That's what most garden fairies do in the winter while their flowers are asleep. But this winter Rosie just hadn't been sleepy, and now the beautiful flower colors had aroused her curiosity. She hadn't seen anything colorful for so long!

The window was opened just wide enough for Rosie to squeeze through. She wasn't worried that she'd be seen. She knew that only adults lived in the house, and adults can't see garden fairies.

3

She landed on the edge of the box and was so surprised at what she saw that she tumbled in, right on top of the bright flowers. But they weren't real flowers – they were flowered clothes! Rosie was amazed. She had seen flowered clothes before, but not like these. In fact, she had never seen flowers like these anywhere.

Suddenly Rosie heard footsteps. She tried to fly away, but before she could move, more clothes landed on top of her. "I've got to get out of here!" she thought.

But just then, the box lid came down and Rosie heard two loud clicks. She was locked in the box.

Someone picked up the box, and Rosie plopped to the bottom of the soft pile of clothes. It was dark, and she could hardly move. Her little heart was pounding. "What have I gotten myself into now?" she thought. "Why didn't I just go to sleep like a sensible fairy?"

Rosie heard people's footsteps hurrying, doors slamming, and a sound she recognized from outdoors: a car engine. The engine noise went on for a long time. The dark box was warm and cozy, and Rosie soon fell asleep, so she didn't notice when the noise changed to the roar of a jet.

Thump! Bump! Rosie woke with a start as the box was thrown open. People were talking and taking things out of the box. Rosie worried that there might be children around, because she knew children could see her. She didn't dislike them – in fact, she loved to hide in the safety of her garden and watch the neighborhood children playing. But she didn't know where she was now, and she didn't want anyone to try to catch her. Oh, how she wished she was home in her garden!

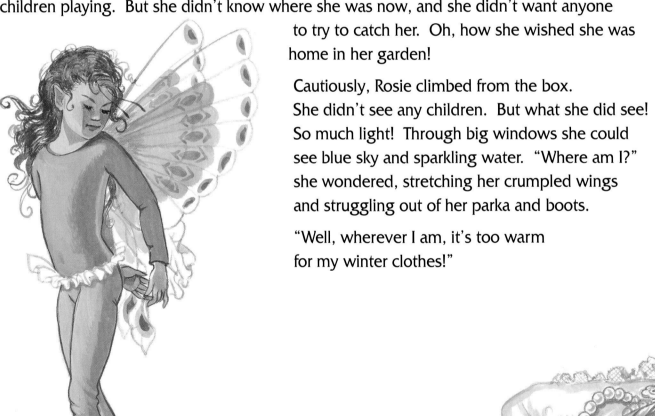

Cautiously, Rosie climbed from the box. She didn't see any children. But what she did see! So much light! Through big windows she could see blue sky and sparkling water. "Where am I?" she wondered, stretching her crumpled wings and struggling out of her parka and boots.

"Well, wherever I am, it's too warm for my winter clothes!"

The man and woman from the house in front of
Rosie's garden were in the room, and the man was
putting on the red and lavender flowers from the box.
A shirt! Rosie had never seen the man wear anything
so wonderful! The woman put on bright-flowered
clothes, too. Then, laughing and talking,
the couple left the room.

Rosie fluttered to a table by the window. She could hardly believe her eyes! There was not a bit of snow, and the sun felt warm on her face.

8

Rosie saw exotic tall trees with huge, swaying leaves. She saw lush green plants and flowers – flowers everywhere! "I must still be asleep!" she thought in amazement.

Eager to be among the colorful flowers, Rosie tried frantically to get out of the room, but the big sliding glass door was too heavy. She paced back and forth impatiently.

Rosie was so busy looking out the window that she didn't notice the couple returning until they had already closed the door.

"Pay attention!" she scolded herself. "You missed a chance to fly out!".

"Isn't Hawaii lovely!" exclaimed the woman.

"Two weeks will go by fast," said the man. "Then we'll be flying back to all that winter."

"Flying?" thought Rosie. "Oh! I guess we came here on an airplane!" She had watched them from her garden. As for Hawaii, she'd never heard of it – but if this was it, she really liked it.

"And I dread the thought of packing those suitcases again," sighed the woman. "Aha!" thought Rosie. "My box was a suitcase!"

"Look at that sunset!" marveled the man, opening the sliding glass door to the balcony.

"Hey," called the man, "do they have hummingbirds in Hawaii?"

"I don't think so," answered his wife.

"Well, I could swear one just flew past my ear!" he said.
"I could hear the whir of its wings!"

Of course, the wings were Rosie's. She flew past his ear, out the glass door, and into the warm, pastel-tinted sunset. "All I need is to be back here in two weeks before my suitcase is closed!" she sang. Giddy with delight, she swooped down toward the garden.

She landed in a tree that had great clusters of beautiful white flowers. They smelled so lovely that she sighed with pleasure.

Then the last golden rays of the sunset faded, and it was night. Rosie snuggled down on a bed of velvety petals and closed her eyes. Her bed was warm, it smelled divine, and just before she drifted off to sleep, she thought to herself that Hawaii was absolutely the nicest place she'd ever imagined.

Rosie woke very early. There were only a few people around.

She took a few sips of dew and splashed some on her face, then set off to explore the garden. As she flew happily from flower to flower, the sun climbed higher and more people began strolling about.

Rosie forgot to watch for children. Suddenly a soft hand grabbed her from behind.

"Mommy! Look what I found!" cried a child's voice. Rosie twisted around as far as she could and looked up in fear. Her captor was a little girl.

"What, Sally?" asked the girl's mother. "I don't see anything."

"It's a fairy, Mommy!" cried Sally. "Look!" She stretched her arm up to show the captured fairy. Rosie tried to stay very still.

"Oh, you're pretending," said Sally's mother.

"She's not pretend!

She's real!" insisted Sally.

"Sally, honey, we'll have to play later,"
said her mother.

"Daddy's waiting. Let's go."
Sally sighed and carefully put Rosie
on a flower. "Well, I can see you,
and I know you're a fairy," she
whispered. "Please don't go away.
I'll be back as soon as I can."

Then she ran after her mother.
Rosie was still shaking. Sally had
seemed sweet enough, but it
terrified her to think of being
captured.

"Shame!" said a little voice by her ear. Rosie almost fell off the flower in surprise.

"You let yourself be caught. Where are you from anyway?" The speaker was a garden fairy no larger than herself, but as exotic-looking as the tropical flowers blooming around them. She was a lovely brown color and had brilliant black eyes shaped like almonds.

"I'm from Vermont, where it's winter," said Rosie.

"Where's Vermont? What's winter?" asked the other fairy.

"It's very far away," answered Rosie, "and winter is a cold time that puts all the flowers to sleep."

"Imagine!" said the brown fairy. "If you've come from far away, you must be a tourist."

"I guess," said Rosie, not having the slightest idea what a tourist was.

"How long are you going to stay?" asked her new friend. Rosie knew the answer to that.

"Two weeks," answered Rosie. "Then it's back home to Vermont."

The other fairy smiled. "Well, Aloha! My name is Ilima. I'm named for a little yellow flower that's used to make Hawaiian leis."

"I'm Rosie, and I guess everyone knows what a rose is," laughed Rosie. She wondered what leis were.

The next few days were happy ones. Ilima taught Rosie about the flowers in the oceanfront garden, and she introduced her to several other garden fairies. They were all very friendly and helpful. None of them had ever heard of a tourist garden fairy, let alone met one, so Rosie was quite a celebrity!

Now and then, Rosie caught a glimpse of the couple from the house in Vermont, and often she saw Sally looking for her. Sally seemed lonely. But getting caught once was quite enough! Besides, Rosie knew the other fairies would be angry if she let Sally see her again.

Very early one morning
Koa, a laughing, brown-eyed boy fairy with beautiful, shimmering red wings, woke Rosie by tickling her nose with a feather.

"Come on Rosie, let's go down to the beach," he said. "You haven't been near the ocean yet, and you shouldn't miss it."

Rosie sat up and stretched. She wasn't sure what going to the beach meant for a garden fairy. But if Koa liked it, it was probably fun.

The two fairies flew hand-in-hand across the garden and over the sandy beach. The sun was just rising, and the Pacific Ocean was a pearly pink and pale blue, the tops of the little wavelets tipped with silver. "Oh!" cried Rosie. "It's almost as beautiful as a flower garden!"

They landed on the sand a few inches from the water.

"Now be careful," warned Koa. "If your wings get wet with this salt water, you won't be able to fly an inch. And if you let yourself get washed into deep water, well, it's 'Goodbye, Rosie!'"

"Oh, I know all about water!"

sang Rosie gaily, as she ran through the foamy bubbles left by a receding wave. "We have a pond in the garden where we play in the summer." She dashed about on the wet sand, making little splashes with her bare feet.

"The ocean is different from ponds," said Koa seriously.

"Oh, nonsense," laughed Rosie. "Water is water!"

Koa began to be sorry that he had brought her to the beach. "Please stay away from the waves," he pleaded.

Suddenly, he flew straight up in the air. "Look out, Rosie!" he shouted.

But Rosie, who had bent over to look at a pretty shell, had her back to the ocean.

At Koa's shout she looked over her shoulder just in time to see a line of white foamy water rushing at her.

21

The next instant she was tumbling in the wave. "Help!" she cried, but all she got was a mouthful of water. Then, just as quickly as it had picked her up, the wave tossed her onto the sand. She wasn't hurt, but what a sad sight she was! Her hair was streaming in her eyes, and her pretty wings were stuck together by the salty water.

"Oh dear, look at my poor wings," moaned Rosie. "How could I have been so foolish? Why didn't you tell me that ocean water moves so quickly?"

Koa just sighed. "It's too late to be sorry now," he said. "We have to get you back to the garden where we can wash your wings so they won't dry as stiff as boards!"

Rosie and Koa looked toward the hotel garden. It seemed miles away. Rosie couldn't fly with her stuck-together wings, and she and Koa could never walk across all that sand on their delicate little feet.

"Perhaps I could carry you," mused Koa.

"No, I'm too heavy for your wings," said Rosie. Then she brightened. "Maybe you and another fairy together could carry me back." Rosie had always been good at solving problems.

"Great idea!" said Koa. "I'll get Carissa." Carissa was the strongest garden fairy. Koa was off with a whir of wings. "Watch out for joggers!" he called back.

22

Rosie had never felt so exposed.

The beach was completely flat, and the damp sand was hard. She couldn't even dig a little ditch in which to hide, so she just sat hugging her knees. She hoped nobody would see or step on her. A few runners did pass by, but they were a safe distance away.

Suddenly, Rosie heard children's voices. Two boys were racing down the beach, yelling and splashing each other with water.

"Hey! What's that?" shouted the older of the boys.

"What? Where?" asked the younger one.

"Right there on the sand. Looks like a flying fish or something!"

The older boy reached out to grab Rosie.

Rosie closed her eyes. "I'm done for," she thought fearfully. But before the boy could grab her, someone else scooped her up, and a familiar voice said...

"This is mine!"

"No way!" cried the older boy. "I saw it first!"

"No you didn't. I've been looking for her for a long time," said Sally. Quickly she thought of something to tell the boys. "It's my doll. I lost her here yesterday."

"It didn't look like a doll. It looked like a fish, and we were going to throw it back into the water," said the boy. Rosie shuddered. The younger boy reached for Sally's hand. "Show us," he demanded.

Rosie lay motionless as Sally opened her hand. She kept her arms and legs stiff and her eyes in a wide-open stare, hoping she looked like a doll.

"Oh, well," said the younger boy. "It is just a doll. You can keep it." With that, the boys went racing up the beach.

Rosie was so relieved that she forgot to be scared. "Oh thank you!" she cried, hugging Sally's thumb. "You saved my life!"

Over Sally's shoulder, Koa and Carissa hovered in shock. It had been bad enough to see Rosie almost caught by those boys, but to see her talking to this girl – it was too much!

"Where have you been?" asked Sally. "I kept looking for you in the garden."

"I've been hiding," Rosie replied. "You just saw what can happen if people see me. But now I need to wash the salt from my wings. Will you please take me to the garden and get me some water?"

"Of course," agreed Sally, and she carried Rosie to the garden as Koa and Carissa fluttered anxiously behind.

"Will you run away?" asked Sally.

"No," promised Rosie. "I'm so stiff, I can barely move."

Sally placed Rosie in a corner of the garden and went to get some water.

The second she was gone, garden fairies seemed to appear from everywhere

"Come on Rosie, we'll carry you," said several of them, trying to grab her hands.

"Hurry! She'll be back soon," urged Koa.

"Come on! Hurry!" they all called, becoming very excited.

"Wait a minute!" said Rosie, shaking loose from their tiny pulling hands.

"I said I'd stay, and I must," she said. "Sally saved me. I can't just disappear!"

"You can't mean that!" "What if she tries to keep you?" "You won't ever get back to your garden in Vermont!" All the tiny voices were calling frantic warnings. Rosie put her hands over her ears.

"Stop!" she insisted. "Nothing like that is going to happen. Just because Sally is different from us doesn't mean she's bad. I trust her. She's just as nice as any of us. You'll see."

Just then they heard Sally's footsteps. All the fairies except
Rosie flew into the shadows. "Don't tell her about us, whatever you do!" they warned.

Sally was carrying a paper cup full of water. Rosie stepped into her hand and turned round and round while Sally gently poured water over her. Soon the sand and salt were gone, and Rosie's wings were unstuck. Then Sally patted Rosie with a little napkin.

"Flap your wings back and forth and they'll dry faster," she suggested. Soon, Rosie's wings were as good as new.

Rosie flew up to Sally's shoulder. "I'm sorry that I hid from you," she said, "but garden fairies are suspicious of humans. We're here to help the flowers, not to be playthings for children."

"I just wanted to be your friend," said Sally sadly. "I would never hurt you."

"I know that now, and of course we can be friends!" exclaimed Rosie. She bounced down from Sally's shoulder and hugged Sally's thumb again, ignoring the horrified little gasps from the surrounding bushes.

In the days that followed, Rosie and Sally spent many happy hours together. Rosie learned a lot about the world outside of gardens, and Sally learned about the flowers and how to tend them.

Rosie's fairy friends still darted away whenever they saw Sally. "She's so big!" said Ilima. "I know she won't let you go home," warned Koa. Rosie wished she could make them see that Sally could be trusted even though she was different from them.

Meanwhile, Rosie was keeping track of her two weeks. For each day she had been in Hawaii, she put a tiny seed in a hole in a branch of her favorite plumeria tree. On the day she put in the fourteenth seed, Rosie sighed, "Sally, today I must leave."

"That's right," said Sally. "I heard the people you came with talking at the hotel pool, and they said they're leaving tonight. You'd better get into your suitcase soon."

It wasn't easy for Rosie and Sally to say goodbye. "I'll miss you so much," said Sally. "I've never had a friend like you."

"Same here," said Rosie. She hugged Sally's thumb, and Sally kissed her gently.

It wasn't any easier for Rosie to say goodbye to her fairy friends.

"It's been wonderful having you here," said Ilima, hugging her.

"Yes," said Koa grinning. "You certainly kept our lives exciting."
Carissa just smiled and squeezed her hand. She looked as if she would cry at any moment.
They had all become very fond of the spirited Rosie.

Each fairy hung a lei of tiny flowers around Rosie's neck and kissed her lightly on the cheek
in what they said was the spirit of Aloha.

Then it was time to go.

"Do you know where your room is?" asked Ilima with a worried frown.

"Oh sure," said Rosie. "I love Hawaii, but I do want to go home, so I made sure I remembered."

Ilima, Koa, and Carissa flew with Rosie to the balcony of the Vermont couple's room. The other fairies stayed in the garden, waving madly. "Come back soon, Rosie!" they called.

As Rosie approached the room, she could see the sliding glass door was open. The man and woman were busy packing their flowery clothes into their suitcases.

Rosie turned back to her friends. "Aloha," she said. "Thank you for everything." Rosie kissed each of her friends on the cheek as they had done to her. Koa turned nearly as red as his wings!

But just as Rosie turned to fly into the room, the man slid the door closed and locked it.

31

"Oh, no!" Rosie cried.

"What will I do now? I can't get in! The people will close their suitcases, and I'll never get home!" The other fairies fluttered around her frantically, but none of them could think of a way to help.

Just then, Ilima caught sight of Sally coming from the beach with her sand bucket and towel. "Maybe Sally will know what to do," she cried, grabbing Rosie by the hand and pulling her toward the little girl.

Sally was surprised to see four little fairies suddenly appear before her.

"Rosie! Why aren't you in your suitcase?" she asked, politely pretending not to see the other three fairies.

"Can you help me?" Rosie pleaded. "The door to the balcony is closed and I can't get in!" Rosie was almost in tears at the thought of never seeing her own garden again.

32

"**Goodness,** you are in trouble," said Sally.

"Do you know the number of your room?"

"No, but it's that one right up there," said Rosie, pointing to the balcony. "One, two, three, four," counted Sally. "It's on the fourth floor, right in the corner. We should be able to find that. Come on." She put all four fairies in her bucket – this was no time to pretend she didn't see Rosie's friends – and rushed into the hotel elevator. She pressed the fourth-floor button and dashed out as soon as the door opened.

"It must be this corner room," she said, running down the carpeted hall.

She stopped and knocked on the door.

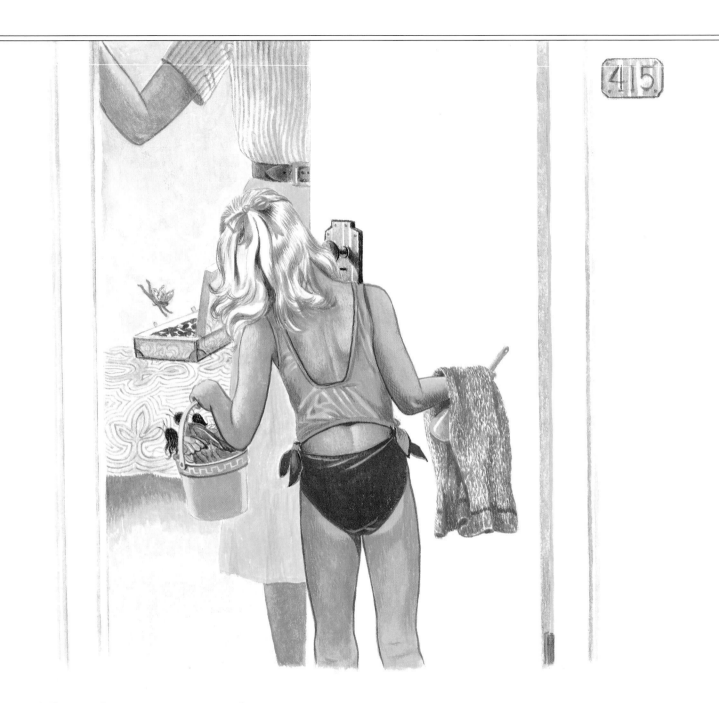

The door opened and the lady from Vermont looked down at Sally.

"This is it!" whispered Rosie joyfully. "Thank you, Sally!" She shot across the room and into the suitcase just seconds before the man shut the lid and snapped the locks.

"Did you come to the wrong room?" the lady asked Sally kindly. Sally peered around her and into the room. When she was sure that Rosie had made it into the suitcase, she looked up and smiled her prettiest smile.

"I guess I did," Sally said. "I must have turned the wrong way when I got off the elevator."

"Hooray!" shouted the fairies. "Rosie was right, you are special, Sally, and a true friend!" They all laughed their twinkling little laughs.

"What an extraordinary laugh that child had," the woman said to her husband as she closed the door.

"Talk about extraordinary!" exclaimed the man. "I could swear I just heard a hummingbird again!"

"Don't be silly," said the lady. "It's just your imagination."

"Well, it's not my imagination that we've had a wonderful vacation!" the man replied. "Let's do this again next year."

"Great," agreed the lady. "We can start planning now!"

Deep in
her soft nest of clothes,

Rosie hugged her tiny flower leis and giggled.
"I bet all my Vermont garden friends
will want to come to Hawaii next year.
I just hope there will be enough room
in the suitcases for us all!"